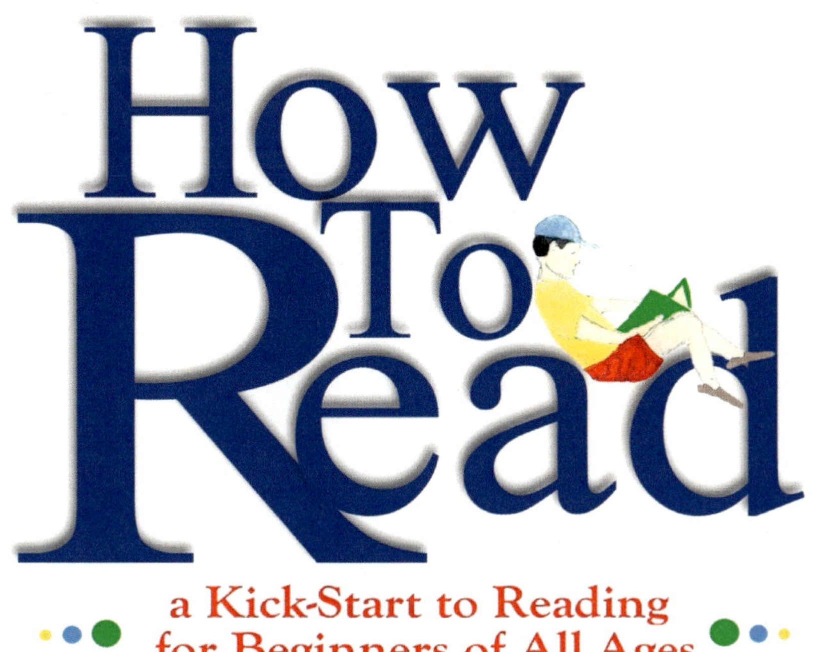

a Kick-Start to Reading for Beginners of All Ages

Written & Illustrated
by
Amy Brotherman
Edited by Carrie Rimmer

Printed in the United States of America.

Cover Design and Illustrations by Amy Brotherman
Edited by Carrie Rimmer

For information, e-mail BadaBee LLC
howtoreadwell@gmail.com

ISBN 978-1-9743-6280-6

BadaBee LLC books may be purchased for personal, educational, business or promotional use. For information on bulk purchases, please contact the author at howtoreadwell@gmail.com or visit createspace.com/howtoread.

To our parents, Dan & Kathy Rimmer,
Thank you for instilling in us a love for reading.
Love, Amy & Carrie

Additional Information for Educators

How to Read is meant for any early reader who is ready to begin the exciting lifetime journey of reading and books. Most students will need to have previous knowledge of many letters and their sounds before beginning the book. It is perfectly fine, however, to begin the lessons even before having a complete grasp of letters and sounds since *How to Read* also incorporates sight reading as part of the learning experience as well as phonics.

Whole language is a method of teaching reading that emphasizes recognizing and memorizing whole words or phrases by sight, seeing the words repeatedly in context, and being immersed in a language-rich environment. The pitfall to this approach is that students rely wholly on memory and become limited by unknown or more difficult words. Therefore, they have difficulty progressing beyond simple reading into advanced reading. The benefits are that students are able to recognize words quickly and are therefore able to read a sentence with more ease, increasing speed, fluency, and comprehension. Many words do not even follow the rules of phonics and so need to be known by sight. Being immersed in a book-rich environment is also a great benefit.

Phonics is a method of teaching that encourages students to first break down words into the "building blocks" of the language into phonemic sounds. Sounds (phonemes) are linked to letters or letter groups, such as vowels (a,e,i,o, or u and sometimes y), consonants (all other letters of the alphabet) or digraphs (the blending of two letters into a single sound). Blends and letter sounds are decoded in the word� and put together to "sound out" the word. The pitfall is that students are laboriously constantly "sounding out" words to read, which can be discouraging and slow. Therefore, speed, fluency, and comprehension may also be slow to come. The benefits are that students are able to decode many unknown words and therefore will be better equipped for advanced reading. Students will also prove to be better spellers and writers because of their firm grasp of phonics.

The beauty and magic of *How to Read* is in the blending of the two methods because truly both are required to become an excellent reader. The method of the book is to introduce a few new words each day. As the student progresses, he repeats the words in review as new ones are brought in. Fairly quickly the lessons incorporate the words into sentences so that the reader is learning context of language and sentence structure. When the reader initially sees a new word, he or she may "sound it out" if desired, or the guiding parent/teacher may speak it to him, and the reader learns the word by sight. *How to Read* encourages ph onics (blends, sounds) and teaches by the repetition an rhyming of other words with similar letters and blends. The author strongly recommends, though, tha at some point, educators should also teach straight phonics in supplement to *How to Read*. We consider *How to Read* to be a "kickoff" of sorts to reading for many students.

May you enjoy the journey and have the opportunity to see
the "light turn on" in the reading of your student!

BEFORE READING:

Before beginning Day One of *How to Read*, the students should:

-know the letters of the English Alphabet (see following page) and most of their sounds.
-have an experienced reader guide them through the pages one day at a time, OR make use of an audio book to understand and practice reading the words.
-view the list of words in the back of this book as a "pre-test" to see how much the student will learn.

Instructions from the teacher before you start:

-The new reader must WANT to learn to read! Encourage a fun reading atmosphere in the home.
-The student should be well rested and ready to begin.
-Learn only one page per day (or two), with review as needed on more difficult previous pages.
-The guide should read the words aloud and then the student will echo. (Or, the student may attempt to sound out the word if he or she wishes.)
-Review the page 3 or 4 times as needed.
-After a reading or two, cover the pictures so the words may be practiced alone.
-If a page is troublesome, stay on it another day or two, but then move on so as not to discourage the reader, returning to it as needed.

Have fun!

In How To Read, the reader will learn:

-125 words including the first 50 Fry "sight words" as seen in the most common sight word lists now used in schools.
-Words of all parts of speech (nouns, verbs, adjectives etc.) to encourage building sentence structure and fluency early in reading.
-Consonant blends and vowel blends
-How to use rhyme in word recognition
-To have an excitement for reading as he or she builds the beginnings of a strong vocabulary day by day!

The Alphabet

Aa Bb Cc Dd

Ee Ff Gg Hh

Ii Jj Kk Ll

Mm Nn Oo

Pp Qq Rr Ss

Tt Uu Vv Ww

Xx Yy Zz

glad

mad

sad

I am

I am mad.

I am sad.

I am glad.

I am sad.

I am mad.

I am glad.

I am sad.

I am mad.

I am sad.

I am glad.

cat

mat

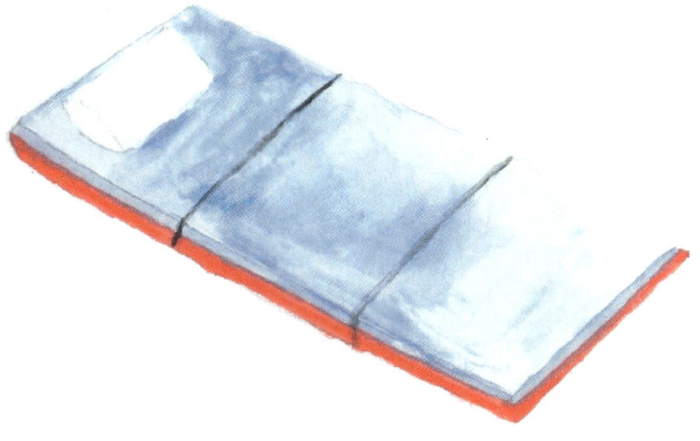

rat

It is a
It is the

It is a cat. It is the rat.

It is a rat. It is the mat.

It is a mat. It is the cat.

It is a cat. It is the rat.

It is a mat. It is the cat.

mail

snail

pail

It is a cat.

It is the rat.

I am mad.

I am sad.

It is a pail.

It is the pail.

It is the mat.

I am a snail.

It is the mail.

I am glad.

It is mad.

I am a cat.

It is a rat.

It is the mat.

It is a mat.

I am glad.

I am sad.

It is the cat.

It is the snail.

The snail is it.

You are.
You are not.

You are glad.

You are not glad.

You are mad.

You are not mad.

You are sad.

You are not sad.

Are you mad?

Are you not glad?

phone

home

I would go.
You should go.

I would go.

You should go.

You should not go.

I go home.

I would go home.

I should go.

Would you go?

Should you not go?

float

throat

coat

This is.
That is.

This is a snail.
That is the mail.
That cat is mad.
This is a coat.
This would float.
That is a rat.
That is the mat.
This is a mat.
That is a throat.
That is a coat.
This cat is glad.

That snail is sad.
This is a rat.
That is a cat.
That cat is sad.
This cat is sad.
This is a pail.
That is a phone.
That should go.
This is home.
That is not home.
This would not float.

He was.
She was.

He was glad.

She was mad.

Was she sad?

Was he glad?

He was a cat.

She was not a cat.

He was not at home.

Was she home?

He was not glad that she was sad.

She was not glad that he was mad.

all

ball

fall

small

This is a ball.

This ball is small.

That ball is small.

The rats all fall.

I would fall.

This ball is not small.

I was not glad that all the balls are small. I was mad that we all would fall.

yours mine

That is yours.

Is this mine?

This coat is yours.

That ball is mine.

It is your throat.

I am glad it is mine.

Is that pail mine?

That is not mine.

one 1

two 2

three 3

One ball is mine.

Two balls are yours.

One, two, three, go!

That is your coat.

The coat is small.

Would you go home?

I was not at home.

One cat is small.

Two cats are not small.

He is a mad snail.

Should the cat fall?

It is the mail.

The three pails are mine.

The sad cat is on the mat.

A mad rat is in the pail.

Two should go in.

This one should go on.

car

far

jar

school

book

This is a school.

Is this your book?

School is far.

Your book is small.

Your car is far.

That phone is small.

The jar on the car is not small.

That is the school.

This is a book in her school.

That is not the small school.

Give me.

Give me the jar.

Give me a small pail.

He should give me a book.

Give me the phone.

She would give me a mat.

Give me your mail.

You should not give me a rat.

Give me a coat.

Give me a small coat.

and

or

This cat is small and mad.

Is it a book, or is it a ball?

Give me a snail and a pail.

Would you float far
on a jar or in a car?

men

pen

hen

They have.

They have two hens.

You have one hen.

They have a small school.

Would you have one coat?

Should you have that ball?

I have a small throat.

They have a rat in a pail.

You have not one car.

They have three mats.

rock

rocks

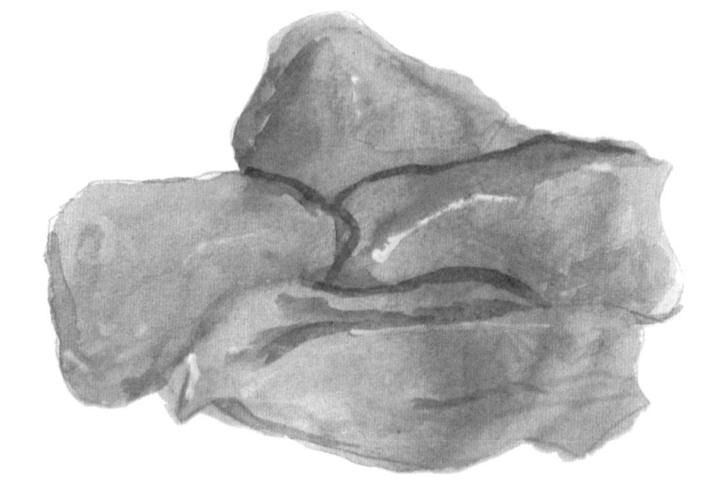

sock

socks

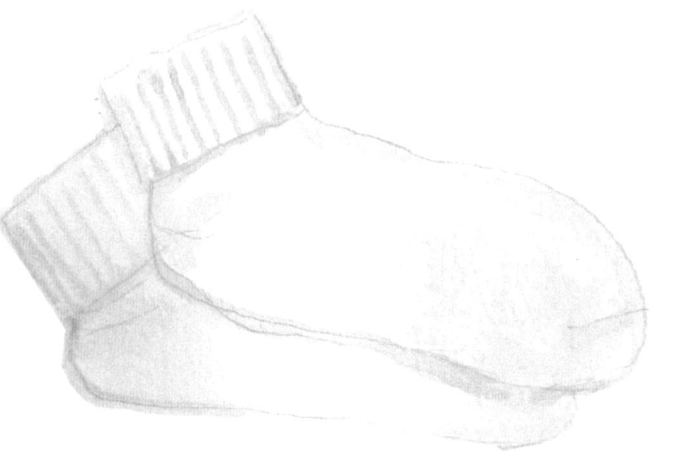

pig

big

dig

wear
tear

I wear the coat.

It is a small tear.

You wear the socks.

The socks have a big tear.

The tear is on the book.

She wears the coat.

Go home and tear the mail.

jeep

sheep

water

milk

juice

That is a milk jar, not a juice jar.

The sheep would not float in the water.

The men in the jeep should have two milk pails.

his
hers

The pen and the book are hers.

The coat and socks are his.

His mail would go in the car.

This phone is hers, and that phone is his.

They have his jar. Would you have hers?

Her mat is on your mat at home.

At school, this book is his.

At home, this book is hers.

mouse

house

blouse

The mouse at his house would not wear a blouse!

to the store
going to the store

They go to the store.

Are you going to the store?

The pig is going to the store.

Go to the store!

Are they going to go to the store?

Am I going to the store?

The socks are at the store.

balloon

soon

moon

We can.

We can go home soon.

We can go far in a balloon.

We can wear a coat.

I am glad we are going in a jeep.

Can we go home?

We can fall on a ball.

Can we tear a coat?

Soon we can mail a book.

The pig can go to the moon.

We can give it water.

We should go in the jeep.

run

jump

will
were

We will jump.

You were far.

Her book will fall.

Were you sad?

He will float.

That one will go.

They were mad.

The cat will jump.

The rat will run.

Will they float?

Were you on a mat? Was the cat mine?

Were you going far? Should the hen fall?

You should not jump on the mail.

Will you go to school? Will you run home?

The snail will float. The rocks were small.

It will not go far.

with

He was with the cat.

The snail is with his pail.

Will you go with your sheep?

The mail is with the men.

He would go with you to dig.

The balloon was with it.

Will we go with the mouse?

We can go home.

I wear the coat.

They go to the store.

The book will fall.

We can go far.

It is a small tear.

Were you sad?

Go to the store!

Can we go home?

You wear her socks.

Soon we can mail a book.

The pig can go to the moon.

We can give it water.

We should go in the jeep.

here

there

Here she is.

There they go.

You go there in his car.

Will you float here?

The moon will go here and there.

put on

puts on

She puts on a coat.

They put on two coats.

The snail put on a sock.

The cat puts on two socks.

She puts on a blouse.

They put it on a house.

He puts it on a rock.

of

off

Give me one of his books.

Go off the mat.

Two of the rocks are far.

It is the mouse of the house.

Jump off the ball!

We run off of the rocks.

hot

cot

dot

my

That is my cot with the dots.

This is a pen of mine.

You should jump off that cot.

This is my ball.

My pail is that one.

My socks have three dots.

That snail is mine.

My balloon will float.

This rock is hot.

Put my socks in the house.

My hen was glad.

My throat is hot.

four 4

five 5

six 6

word

number

This is the number five.

Were all the words in the book?

That is the number four.

She put the word in her book.

One, two, and three are numbers.

This word is on the phone.

Soon they will have six cots.

Four, five, and six are not all that big.

Jump off the jeep!

from

The cat was from the store.

I am from this house.

Are you from that school?

The snail will float in the pail.

I would go from here.

She would go from there.

The men will fall from the jeep.

The sheep will run from there.

guitar

piano

drum

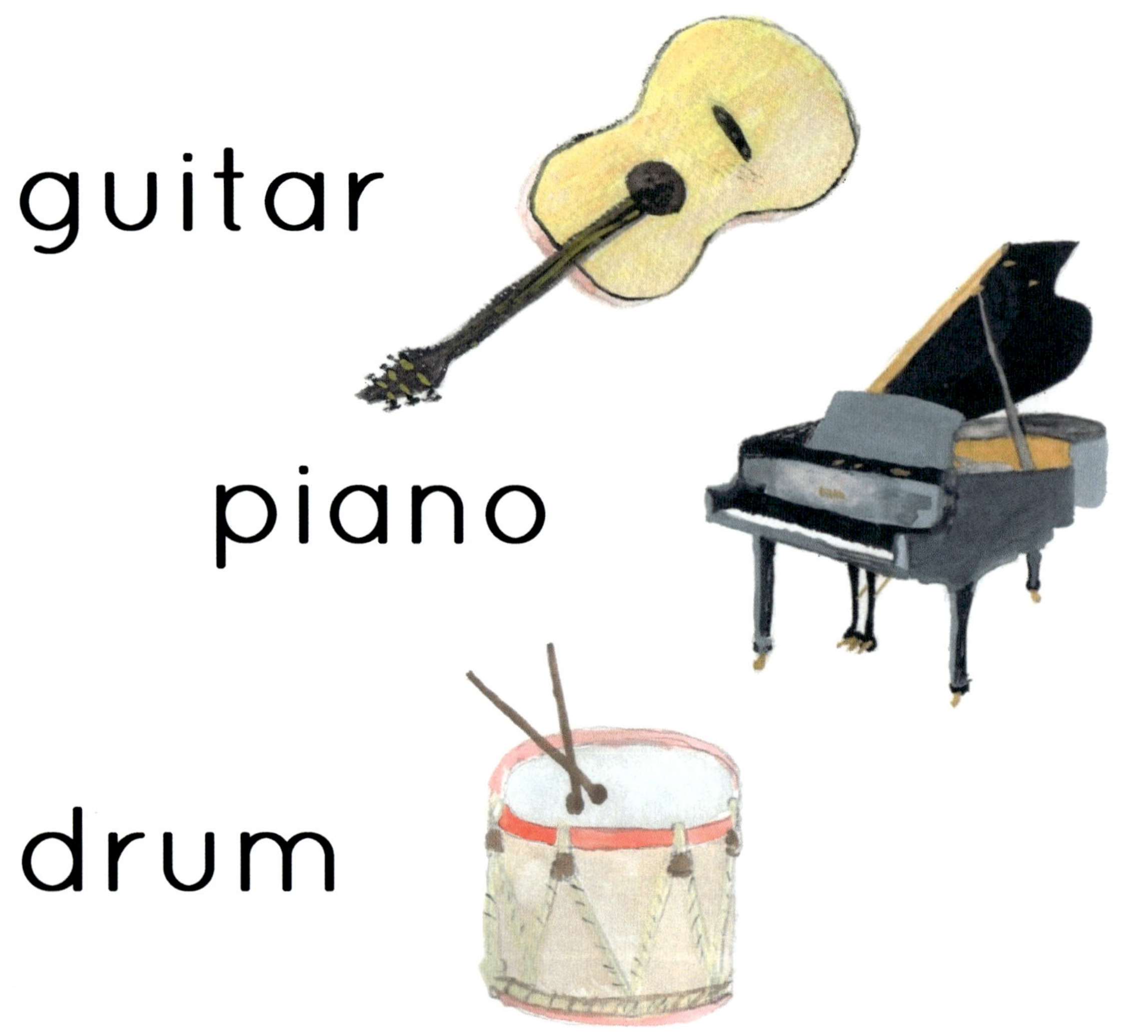

It is a guitar, a piano, and a drum.

Six drums are yours, and one piano is mine.

I have four guitars at my school.

by

She will run by the school.

The pig will dig by the rock.

He puts the socks by the coat.

He will have the guitar and the drums by the piano.

Number one is by number two.

The pen is by his book.

so many
so much

There are so many balloons!

They can run so much.

So many rocks are hot.

I have so much.

You have so much milk, and not much juice.

Too many sheep are here.

Here are so many men.

Should they have so much?

Would this blouse have many dots?

There are so many rocks on the cot.

fish

dish

There are five or six fish on the dish.

Fish and dish are not big words.

look at

Look at the guitar and the drums.

Look at the sad snail!

The fish will look at the dish.

Look at the big moon.

Look at the small rock.

I will look at the book.

The mouse will look at his house.

You should not look at the rat.

I would look at the water in the dish.

They come.
It is coming.

They come here.

It is coming there.

They come to the store.

It is coming to the school.

Three or four fish come here soon.

A hen will come by.

A fish is coming to look at the dish.

quick
quickly

They come here quickly.

Are you coming here quickly?

The cat will run quickly.

Quick! Are you going to give me juice or milk?

Were they quick to go to school?

The quick pig will fall in the water.

for

That piano is for you.

Is that book for me?

The mouse will run for the house.

Go dig for a snail.

The phone is for you.

Would you run for it?

They go to jump for a balloon.

It is so soon for this big moon.

All for one, and one for all!

up

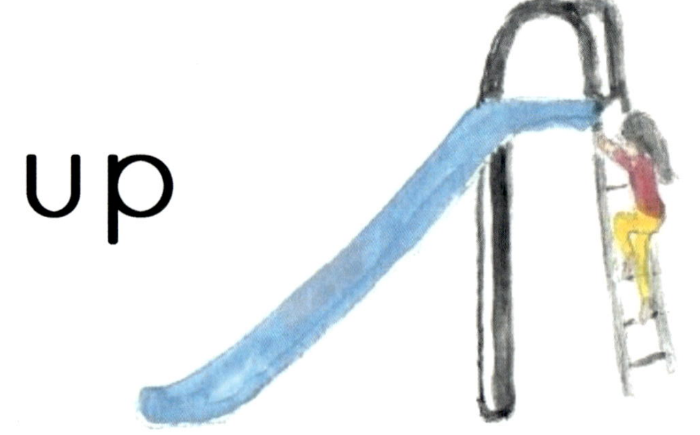

down

Put the dish down.

The six fish are down in the water.

The men put up the drums and guitar.

A piano is down by the house.

Up, up, up, float all these balloons.

each
which

Each one is coming.

Which number is here?

Each phone is for you.

Which rock will float?

I will wear each coat.

Which sheep is it?

Which should I have?

Each balloon will float.

They each come quickly.

Which of the men will go home?

gold

cold

fold

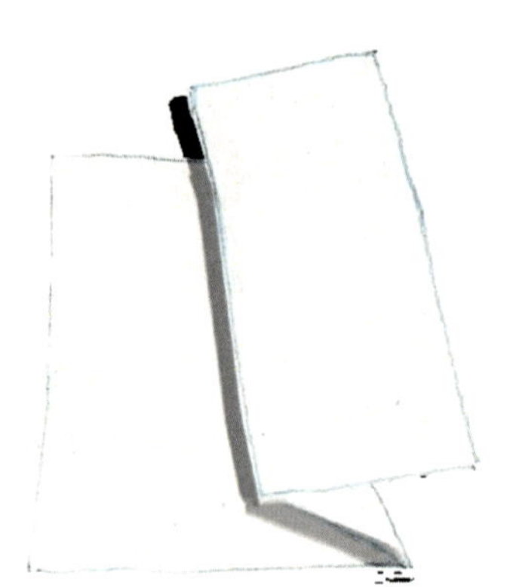

It is her jar of gold.

There are five or six gold rocks in each jar.

The cold juice is down your throat.

We should fold the blouse.

Come and fold two socks.

Put down three or four gold pens.

Was the milk cold or hot?

That is all, and so you are off!

We want to congratulate you
for finishing the book!

Follow us on Facebook and Twitter:

How to Read: a Kick-Start to Reading for Beginners of All Ages

Great job!

Words in *How To Read*
* Fry Words

glad
mad
sad
I*
am
cat
mat
rat
it*
is*
a*
the*
mail
snail
pail
you*
are*
not*
phone
home
would*
go*
should
gloat
throat

coat
this*
that*
he*
was*
she*
all*
ball
fall
small
yours*
mine
one*
two*
three
on*
in*
car
far
jar
school
book
give
me
and*

or*
men
pen
hen
they*
have*
rock(s)
sock(s)
pig
big
dig
wear
tear
jeep
sheep
water*
milk
juice
his*
hers*
mouse
house
blouse
to*
store
going

balloon
soon
moon
we*
can*
run
jump
will*
were*
with*
here
there*
put(s)
of*
off
hot
cot
dot
my*
four
five
six
word*
number*
from*
guitar

piano
drum
by*
so*
many
much
fish
dish
look*
at*
come*
coming
quick
quickly
for*
up*
down*
each*
which*
gold
cold
fold

Made in the USA
Monee, IL
08 March 2022